The Fool's Journey through the Tarot
~ Major Arcana ~

Book 1
The Fool's Journey
Series

by

Noel Eastwood

3rd Edition 2018

IMPORTANT LEGAL NOTICE

This story is a work of fiction. The contents of this book are in no way a substitute for personal supervision or treatment by a qualified medical or psychological professional. The author, editors and publishers accept no responsibility for outcomes if you use the techniques described in this book.

3rd Edition ©Noel Eastwood 2018

Apart from any fair use for the purposes of private study, research, criticism or review no part may be reproduced without written permission of the author.

Please direct all communication to the author, Noel Eastwood.
Email: info@plutoscave.com

Tarot deck: Original Waite-Smith (1910)
Excerpts: *The Pictorial Key to the Tarot* by Arthur Edward Waite (1911)
Cover design and photographs: JoAnn
Map: Damijan

Acknowledgements

I would like to thank my wonderful team of supporters. Most importantly, thank you to my wife, Marja, for her selfless care and loving support. Thank you to my Wordmage, Kristal. A special thank you to Mark, Michael, Steven and Lorna for helping with the first edition of this book. A heartfelt thank you to JoAnn for her generous editing and cover for the 3rd edition. JoAnn brings a wealth of experience in the personal growth field and it is a pleasure to work closely with someone who understands my work so well.

Dedication

To my three children, Sonja, Michael and Steven. You taught me more about life than I would ever have learned without your love and support.

Contents

Map of the Tarot Empire
Introduction to the 3rd Edition 2018
The Fool
The Magician
The High Priestess
The Empress
The Emperor
The Hierophant
The Lovers
The Chariot
Strength
The Hermit
Wheel of Fortune
Justice
The Hanged Man
Death
Temperance
The Devil
The Tower
The Star
The Moon
The Sun
Judgement
The World
Epilogue
About the author

Introduction to the 3rd Edition

When I wrote the first edition of this book I wanted to expand on the rich symbolism of The Fool by exploring his relationship with the Major Arcana archetypes. Since then, it has become a popular book with Tarot enthusiasts and practitioners alike.

It has also attracted a wider audience amongst those interested in personal growth. I have expanded this Third Edition to include material that I believe will satisfy these readers as well.

There are many excellent books on the history of the Tarot and on interpretations of the cards, particularly those of the Major Arcana. My contribution to the existing literature is an allegorical novella in which The Fool's Journey through the Tarot becomes a mystic's journey. It follows Follin's inner journey of discovery and his search for knowledge through direct experience with the Tarot archetypes.

I wrote it in fictional form to make it more readable than a recipe book of Tarot card meanings. It includes interpretations I use in my readings and draws on my encounters with the Tarot archetypes during my meditations with their cards.

The Waite-Smith deck illustrated by Pamela Colman Smith was chosen for the simplicity and clarity of her images and their ease of translation into meaning. Also, many of the more modern Tarot decks stem from the Waite-Smith deck which is easily accessible to all.

In this Third Edition, Follin's journey contains more detail than previously, including additional interaction with the Tarot archetypes. It no longer includes explanatory notes, apart from Arthur Waite's original card descriptions. This third edition has been extensively edited and is much better for it.

It is important to note that there is more to the Fool's journey than the Major Arcana. The four suits (Pentacles, Swords, Cups and Wands) were calling me to give them a voice, so I have. *The Fool's Journey through the Tarot Pentacles* and *The Fool's Journey through the Tarot Swords* are now published with *Cups* and *Wands* to be completed later in 2018.

They take the story of Follin's growth much farther and deeper as he interacts with each of the Minor Arcana. I have taken the liberty to delay the introduction of The Fool's dog until later in the series. You will meet his fae pup in Book 2, as Follin journeys through the Pentacles Kingdom.

The choice of interpretation for each card is mine alone. Each Tarotist has his or her own preferences and this will show in differences in reading style and interpretation. This reflects the broad diversity of Tarot imagery, symbolism and the vagaries of the human experience.

Noel Eastwood
May 2018

"The true Tarot is symbolism; it speaks no other language and offers no other signs. Given the inward meaning of its emblems, they do become a kind of alphabet which is capable of indefinite combinations and makes true sense in all."

Arthur Edward Waite *The Pictorial Key to the Tarot* (1911).

The Fool

Innocence; folly; spontaneity; faith; trust; beginning.

"The fool doth think he is wise, but the wise man knows himself to be a fool."

William Shakespeare, *As You Like It*

From The Pictorial Key to the Tarot A.E. Waite (1911)

"With light step, as if earth and its trammels had little power to restrain him, a young man in gorgeous vestments pauses at the brink of a precipice among the great heights of the world; he surveys the blue distance before him - its expanse of sky rather than the prospect below... He is a prince of the other world on his travels through this one ... amidst the morning glory, in the keen air. The sun, which shines behind him, knows whence he came, whither he is going, and how he will return by another path after many days. He is the spirit in search of experience."

~

Along a dusty dirt road in the countryside of the Mystic Isle a youth is walking. He steps out lightly with laughter in his throat and a bright smile on his face. Having left his home and family troubles behind he feels happy, carefree. He effortlessly strides through the countryside for miles and miles.

As he passes the dry stubble of a harvested wheat field he spies an old scarecrow. He climbs through the timber-railed fence and, stepping carefully over the cut wheat stalks, walks over to the scarecrow.

The scarecrow's clothes are old, the shirt is thin and well worn. It has many ragged holes in it. The Fool gently and carefully, almost reverently, removes the shirt and places it on the ground. Then he takes his own shirt off and puts it respectfully on the scarecrow as though he is dressing his aged grandfather. He steps back, chuckles to himself and puts the scarecrow's worn shirt on his own back and returns to the road.

Later that day, weary and beginning to question the wisdom of his flight from home, the boy finds himself on the edge of the sea cliffs. He puts down his staff and bundle and peers over the edge at the waves crashing below. He stands up again, takes up his staff and bundle and moves on.

~

The group across the channel observes him, pointing him out to those amongst them who had not yet noticed the boy.

"Do we turn him back?" one asks.

"Is he too young?" another adds.

"Is he ready?" from another.

"What do we know of him?" from yet another.

"Ah, 'tis young Follin, native of the Mystic Isle," one of the elders explains. "Fourteen years old. He is but a boy and the burdens at home are such that even his father could not face them."

"So he runs..." another chimes in.

"Just as his father did," says another.

"No, the father ran from failure of his powers, a mixture of pride, guilt and grief. The boy runs from inadequacy and shame. The burden is too great for his young shoulders. He has not yet come to believe in himself. Reflected in the eyes of his family, peers, teachers and elders he sees himself a fool."

"Untapped potential," another murmurs.

"Shall we take him on then?" asks one of the voices.

"But is he too damaged?" questions another.

"Yes, he is disturbed, depressed and sees no future for himself," comes the reply. "He is naive, bullied at school, dyslexic and ignorant of the world beyond..."

"We see his folly, his ignorance, his stumbling and we must ask ourselves: This poor Fool, will he ever succeed in life?" another intones.

Their voices weave through the group: a whisper of wind, a hiss; a grunt of assent; a rising inflection, melodic and true.

"Do we do this for his benefit, his enlightenment, or is it to fulfil our own needs?" another queries.

Suddenly the group turns as one. The boy had jumped from the cliff, or had he just fallen? His body plummets towards the rocks below, still clutching his staff and bundle. Before his feet touch the waves a rainbow appears beneath his feet. His downward momentum ceases and he is propelled forward along the rainbow as if it were a bridge.

The group across the channel disappears and a solitary figure strides down to the shoreline to meet the boy.

~

Follin steps off the rainbow bridge onto the mainland. He

naively walks his own path, not knowing where his journey may take him.

Carrying his belongings in a cloth sack, wrapped about a stout staff, he remembers not, nor cares, what it contains. It is just another burden he has to carry through life, or so he thinks. *'Just like the bullying at school and the colour of my hair. Like the shame of having a sick mother I had to care for when I was supposed to be studying. Like my father who left when my brother died. Life is a mystery - and a burden.'*

~

Follin begins his journey as a naive fool but it will soon become a journey of discovery into himself. Leaving behind all he knows, and ignorant of the consequences of his actions, Follin begins a mystic's journey. Like so many Fools before him, his is a quest for wisdom, knowledge, enlightenment, but he does not know it yet.

The Magician

Conscious mind; action; initiating a project; power of the mind.

From <u>The Pictorial Key to the Tarot</u> A.E. Waite (1911)

"This... shews the descent of grace, virtue and light, drawn from things above and derived to things below. The suggestion throughout is therefore the possession and communication of the Powers and Gifts of the Spirit. On the table in front of the Magician are the symbols of the four Tarot suits, signifying the elements of natural life, which lie like counters before the adept, and he adapts them as he wills."

~

Along the winding path from the mainland shore Follin encountered a Magician, the Master of the Four Elements. Mage Hermes, The Emperor's Magician and alchemist, smiled at the young man knowingly, recognising something of his own youthful folly.

He asked Follin if he could look into the bag wrapped about his staff. Then, in grand fashion, The Magician raised one arm to the skies, and, with the other, pointed to the ground. With a flash of light and the sound of thunder, Follin's bag opened. The Magician withdrew several items from his own bag, one by one. These are gifts of great importance, for the mage knows that Follin will need them later on his journey through the four Kingdoms of the Tarot Empire.

From his own bag Mage Hermes drew forth a plain yet beautifully crafted dagger, explaining as he handed it carefully to Follin: "This dagger will cut a man's head off as easily as it will expose the treachery in his mind. It is of Air and will help bring clarity to your thinking and help you discern truth."

Next Mage Hermes drew forth a flaming Wand, saying: "This is born of Fire. It will assist in developing your creativity and foster in you a taste for adventure." Follin gratefully accepted the Wand, quickly realising that although it flamed it did not burn what it touched. As he placed it carefully into his bag he saw it grow dim.

Then followed a golden Coin, "This gift of Earth will remind you that all you gain in life must be earned through determination and steadfast resolve."

Finally The Magician handed Follin a turquoise Cup. "Each time you drink from this cup you will be reminded of the power and importance of love and compassion. Without these qualities life holds no meaning."

Staring in awe at The Magician and his gifts, yet ignorant of their worth, Follin stammered, "Thank you, my Lord".

The mage leaned towards Follin. "To understand these precious gifts requires selfless, dedicated effort. All those who journey along the mystic's path must first earn the right to wield their gifts of power. These gifts will guide you along your journey - learn their worth and use them wisely. With discipline and practice you will find yourself a Master upon the wheel of life, then you will no longer need them. At which time you, yourself, may gift them to another Fool starting out on his journey."

"Now, before I leave you, do you have any questions for me?"

"Yes." Follin paused. He did not want to appear ignorant before such an august personage but he felt he must ask: "Who... who are you?"

The mage smiled. "Well, I am real, if that is what you are getting at. I am Mage Hermes, a teacher of science, writing, religion and magic. I use a practical form of magic, uniting heaven and earth to manifest ideas in physical form."

Mage Hermes continued "You think that you are running away but now you are on the path to self-discovery. You have much to learn. Although I can see that you have the courage to confront your fears, you will not walk alone."

The mage stepped back, smiling as he swirled his cloak around him, and Follin was alone once more.

Smiling with delight at Mage Hermes' gifts, Follin gathered up his bag, and, with a whistle on his lips and a skip in his step, he continued along his way. Far from home, he was now in the Tarot Empire.

The High Priestess

Intuition; silence; inner worlds; unconscious; secret; mystery; the unknown.

From <u>The Pictorial Key to the Tarot</u> A.E. Waite (1911)

"The scroll in her hands is inscribed with the word Tora, signifying the Greater Law, the Secret Law and the second sense of the Word. It is partly covered by her mantle, to shew that some things are implied and some spoken. She is seated between the white and black pillars - J and B - of the mystic Temple, and the veil of the Temple is behind her... There are some respects in which this card is the highest and holiest of the Greater Arcana."

~

One evening as Follin wandered through the forest he came across a dense glade of ferns and flowering lilies. There he spied a stunningly beautiful woman, Hera, The High Priestess. She was standing between black and white pillars, illuminated by the glow of the moon. He approached with awe as she summoned him to come closer.

"Young man, I see you are a wanderer. Where have you come from and what have you learned in your life thus far?" she asked softly, so softly that Follin strained to hear her. Not wanting to disappoint this beautiful woman he explained as much as he could before he lost his confidence.

"Madam, I am from the village of Saoirse, it means, 'be true to yourself'. Saoirse rests on the edge of the Mystic Isle's southern forests. My father is a respected mage and healer. He was the Mage of Saoirse, but when he lost my older brother to the plague something happened to him. One day he just got up and left. My mother said that he felt such grief at failing to cure his son that he had to find himself all over again. My mother forgave him, she was wonderful back then. I tried to help my mother and little sister. I hunted and foraged for food in the forest. I tried to study hard to make my mother proud. I always did my best but I am a failure. I struggle to read and write, I hardly know my numbers and only a few days ago I tried to... I decided to leave home and find my father or maybe it was to find myself, I really don't know what I was doing."

The High Priestess Hera nodded sagely. Follin relaxed when he saw the look of understanding and compassion in her eyes. She encouraged the youth to open the bag sitting between his feet. When he opened the cloth Mage Hermes' four elemental gifts spilled onto the forest floor. Follin quickly gathered them back into his arms, holding each gently as he explained his story.

"Madam, these were gifted to me by the Mage Hermes. He said

that I should learn to use them, yet I don't know how," he sighed.

Silently The High Priestess lifted two paper scrolls from her lap and handed them to the youth.

"Through solitude and the diligent study of these scrolls, you will earn what you seek," she said in such a soft whisper that Follin had to lean forward to place his ear close to The High Priestess' mouth. Hera had deliberately pitched her voice soft and low. She wanted the youth to learn to pay careful attention when people spoke to him.

Follin was somewhat puzzled by her words. He doubted that he would be able to fulfil The Priestess' wishes. Follin's schooling had always been troublesome and he remained traumatised by the beatings and humiliation that drove him to embark on this dangerous journey. Well he knew that his ability to read was poor; he struggled to communicate his thoughts clearly just as he struggled to focus and attend when people spoke to him.

It was The High Priestess' objective to introduce Follin to the art of meditation.

"Follin, are you sitting comfortably?" she asked.

When Follin nodded she continued. "Close your eyes. Bring your awareness to your breathing. Feel the flow of air into and out of your nostrils." She paused.

"When thoughts or feelings arise, gently return your awareness to your breath... in and out... It is tempting to follow your thoughts and feelings like rabbits down a burrow. When you become aware that your focus has wandered gently return your attention to your breathing."

The High Priestess watched as Follin's thoughts and feelings flitted across his face. She could see when his attention wandered and could tell when he returned his attention to his breathing.

"Return your attention to your breath" she prompted several

times.

The High Priestess then asked Follin to let go of his focus on his breath. "Follin, keeping your eyes closed become aware of your body and the sounds around you. Sit quietly for a few moments, then open your eyes slowly and return your attention to the here and now."

Follin camped for some time near The High Priestess' Sanctuary and almost every night she invited him to join her to continue his meditation training.

Sometimes towards the end of his breath meditation, Hera would softly invite Follin to place his awareness on different parts of his body until he felt a letting go. Other times she invited him to turn his attention to an external object. Follin's favourite was to focus on one of the plants in Hera's Sanctuary, to feel its texture, smell its perfume, taste its nectar, hear the sound of the breeze as it passed through its leaves, and to see its colours change through all colours of the rainbow.

By day Follin read the scrolls and studied Mage Hermes' gifts. When Follin visited The High Priestess Hera they meditated together. Afterwards, when he fell asleep, Hera taught the youth as he sat at her feet in his dream body.

Follin found that these periods of solitude and study did something to his mind. When he dreamed with The High Priestess his senses were heightened. Where before his mind would wander, when he was in Hera's Sanctuary he could remain fully focused. He found that in this state of altered consciousness he could attend closely to everything she said.

Follin recognised that there was something magical about Hera's Sanctuary but could not quite grasp what. Her Sanctuary was as beautiful as The High Priestess herself, yet it was not quite as healthy as he felt it could be.

Follin spent each day reading and rereading the scrolls but

continued to struggle with his confidence to understand what he read. The youth was so afraid of making a mistake that he could barely hear The High Priestess' voice in his head when she spoke to him.

'Trust your intuition,' he heard when his confidence waned.

One evening The High Priestess bid Follin farewell. He was reluctant to leave as he still did not understand the scrolls. He could make out the individual words but they did not make sense to him. He did not want to admit that to her. As he sadly left her Sanctuary he heard her whispered voice in his mind, *'Go softly, go gently.'*

As Follin wandered through the forest he reflected on his time with The High Priestess. He had learned to calm his mind and to enter her Sanctuary in his dream body. It was this state, out-of-body, that she succeeded in tutoring him in the art of astral travel.

Through solitude and silence The High Priestess had also given him precious gifts of meditation and dreaming. These were all very valuable tools for his mystic's journey.

She had also given him the scrolls but he had yet to understand their true purpose.

As he sat tending his campfire alongside the quiet forest path that evening, Follin thought to himself, *'Perhaps if I continue to practise mental stillness ... calm ... solitude ... silence ... meditation ... dreaming ... one day I will be able to interpret her secret scrolls ... to unlock the meaning of The Magician's gifts'* he thought as he continued his journey.

The Empress

Fertility; sexuality; abundance; mother; maternal warmth; balance; harmony.

From The Pictorial Key to the Tarot A.E. Waite (1911)

"The symbol of Venus is on the shield which rests near her. A field of corn is ripening in front of her, and beyond there is a fall of water... She is the inferior Garden of Eden, the Earthly Paradise, all that is symbolised by the visible house of man... In another order of ideas, the card of the Empress signifies the door or gate by which an entrance is obtained into this life, as into the Garden of Venus..."

~

Follin wandered through thick, forested hills until he came across a large stone castle. The rain that had been looming all day began to fall heavily. Fearful that he would soon be drenched, Follin hammered on the castle gates until they opened. A tall guard greeted him and took him to meet The Empress.

On first appearance, the youth thought her a frighteningly powerful-looking woman. As he stood dripping water onto the stone floor he noticed that not only was she beautiful, she was also very alluring. He felt an arousal he had not known before, a desire for love, affection and other feelings that confused him.

The Empress ordered tea and cake to be brought and together they sat in front of a roaring fire. She asked him what he was carrying in his bag, carefully stowed at his feet. Follin looked directly into The Empress' eyes and, intuitively knowing he could trust her, told her everything that had happened on his journey thus far.

"Young man, these are special gifts indeed," said The Empress as she examined the four elemental pieces and the two scrolls. "We all carry gifts through life," she explained, "but only those who make the effort to cultivate inner balance and harmony will ever learn to use them. These objects, gifted by Mage Hermes and High Priestess Hera, are of limited value without knowing their secrets. But first, I would like to teach you one way to access your personal power."

With a seductive look in her eyes she proceeded to teach Follin the art of balance and harmony in walking. The Empress called it 'centred walking'.

"The mystic walks softly and gently so as to always be ready to move and act. His feet remain grounded, his will is allowed to grow with each step. He is aware of his energy connection with the ground beneath him. The mystic walks like this to generate personal power in his physical body and to strengthen his will."

The Empress then took Follin to a large circle drawn in the courtyard. As she walked around the circle's circumference, pointing her hands inwards, she explained, "I step first on the ball of my foot before I ground my heel," she said. "Now you try it."

Follin practised each day to walk the circle like a mystic, to walk 'softly, gently'. At first, it was hard not to put the heel of his foot down first, very hard, but once he learned to slide his toes forward, just above the ground before placing his foot down, he found it became easier.

There were other tasks for him besides walking in circles. Follin fetched water for the kitchen staff and wood for their stoves. He was up before dawn and at midday he would join several journeymen from other Tarot Kingdoms in a meal, followed by meditation. Fortunately, the inner silence techniques he had learned from High Priestess Hera ensured he was refreshed by the time their break was over. Then it was more work in the fields to pull weeds and help in the vegetable gardens. Each evening he would study Hera's scrolls and listen to The Empress' words of wisdom.

"All things that exist in harmony are one with life, the flow of Yin and Yang. When you are 'at one with the flow', on the path of the mystic, you can move the 'change-point' in others. This might be as a healer; in self-defence; or in their spiritual development. Spend time each day walking the circle feeling your personal power, and you will better understand the scrolls which my sister, Hera, gave you. You will also learn more about how to use the gifts from my brother, Hermes." Follin practised centred walking every day but the deeper understanding of the scrolls still eluded him.

Through the Empress' exercises Follin learned to flow with his body movements which helped develop his internal harmony. He learned the power of patience and to use his senses consciously to explore and engage with the world around him.

For a youth who had struggled with self-esteem issues throughout childhood; who was bullied by his bigger school mates; beaten by his teachers because he could barely read or write; a young man who spent more time sitting in the Dunce's Corner in class than in his own seat; these lessons certainly were a challenge.

Follin diligently practised his centred walking. In time, he could feel his centre of personal power - behind his navel. He found The Empress' exercises gave him confidence in his ability to perform the tasks he was set by the kitchen staff. The young Mystic Islander could now balance his mind while gently flowing his body from one posture to another as he walked.

How long he was in the castle Follin did not know, having lost count of the days filled with work, meditations and the lessons from The High Priestess.

One day he woke to find everyone gone. The castle was empty, the walls covered in vines and weeds. As he gathered his belongings together he heard The Empress' voice, *'Remember, what goes around comes around, everything is a circle, like the cycle of birth, death, rebirth. Follow your path, young Follin.'*

He thanked the emptiness around him with a genuine sadness in his voice. He then left the castle to find a path leading into the forest to continue his journey.

The Emperor

Power; rules; boundaries; father; authority; responsibility.

From <u>The Pictorial Key to the Tarot</u> A.E. Waite (1911)
"He is a crowned monarch - commanding, stately, seated on a throne, the arms of which are fronted by rams' heads. He is executive and realization, the power of this world, here clothed with the highest of its natural attributes. He is the virile power, to which the Empress responds."

~

Follin now had some tools, some knowledge, and, most of all, some patience to perform the tasks set by his mentors to continue his learning by himself. He found that he enjoyed walking along the forest paths, making camp late each afternoon. After his dinner he would try to read the scrolls by firelight but, though the words were clear, he still could not discern their meaning. Sometimes he dreamed, sometimes not. Each morning he practised the techniques he had been taught and during the day used his centred walk, except when he forgot or was distracted.

~

One day he emerged from the forest to find himself back at the castle. Scratching his head he turned this way and that, yet there it was, it indeed was the same castle. He then recalled The Empress' parting words, *'Remember, what goes around comes around, everything is a circle...'*

Follin pounded heavily on the gate but suddenly stopped when the gates flew open and a powerfully built man strode purposely towards him. Follin noticed the man was richly dressed and a long sword swung at his side.

The Emperor reached forward to grasp Follin's hand in his. "Welcome back. I believe you've already met my wife, The Empress. She speaks very highly of you, of your integrity, your honesty and your dedication to the mystic's path. Please, come and meet my staff. I have some lessons of my own to teach you." The Emperor shivered in the cool afternoon air. "I believe you and I need some exercise to warm ourselves on this chilly day."

Together Follin and The Emperor chatted with the stable hands as horses were saddled for them. They were soon riding through the forest, along dark paths and across grassy fields. As they rode The Emperor explained how much he loved his Empire; of how little time he had available to care for the land, the people and the gods who resided there.

He carefully explained to Follin that it was the laws, and the indomitable strength of his character to uphold those laws compassionately, which kept the Empire alive and safe for his people.

"It's not just law and order, but skill and bravery; the creativity to develop strategic boundaries; and then to be prepared to enforce and defend them. People without boundaries always complain they are being cheated. They are never satisfied when they have enough, always wanting more - generally more of what belongs to others."

From high on a grassy hilltop The Emperor waved his hand across the landscape before them. "Son, one day you will help me keep this kingdom safe; when you can set your own boundaries and be able to defend them successfully from those who lack the willpower, wisdom and courage to manage themselves."

Follin doubted that he had heard aright. He looked carefully at The Emperor. "Sire, how do I learn about boundaries, laws and rules? I thought mighty rulers had soldiers to enforce and defend their boundaries. I didn't know individuals could set boundaries for themselves."

The Emperor explained that when Follin had been with The Empress he had learned about personal power and about the day to day running of the castle. "Now it is time for you to experience it from a broader perspective, to learn to rule one's self and to lead others wisely."

For an hour or two each day The Emperor kept Follin by his side as he dealt with the many problems that were presented to him. Follin observed as The Emperor met delegations from the kingdoms, adjudicated disputes between his own people, wrote letters, made decisions or pondered affairs of state. The Emperor would patiently explain his reasons for his actions and answer Follin's numerous questions.

Although still a naive youth and scarred from years of misery and trauma at his school, Follin watched and listened as best he could. His sessions at the feet of The High Priestess and The Empress made it easier for him to sit quietly in contemplation after each lesson.

Follin became aware that The Emperor took into account all parties' needs and his decisions were based on the greatest good, and not on his own wealth, comfort or whim. He also observed The Emperor's patience, compassion and firmness; his dignity and self-discipline.

After several months The Emperor left to visit the Wands Kingdom in the northeast where border disputes had escalated.

It was time for Follin to return to the solitude of the forests.

The Hierophant

Teacher; culture; tradition; conservative; learning.

From The Pictorial Key to the Tarot A.E. Waite (1911)

"He has been usually called the Pope, which is a particular application of the more general office that he symbolizes. He is the ruling power of external religion, as the High Priestess is the prevailing genius of the esoteric, withdrawn power."

~

One afternoon as he was about to stop and prepare his evening meal and then sleep, Follin came face to face with an old man. The grandfatherly man introduced himself as The Hierophant, a High Priest of the Tarot Empire. He appeared the embodiment of wisdom and tradition. His manner was of a conservative style familiar to Follin. This wise old man reminded him of his father, the Mage of Saoirse.

Together they gathered firewood, for the weather had turned cold. Having walked for many days without seeing anyone, Follin wanted to talk, to pour out the story of his adventures. Sensing he could trust this calm, quiet gentleman, Follin hurriedly built a warm fire and set his pot of water to boil for their meal, and afterwards, for their cup of tea.

When the water had boiled Follin gasped in admiration: The Hierophant had picked the pot of boiling water from the fire with his bare hands, without flinching.

"How did you do that, sir?" gasped the youth.

"I have lived through many ages and I have learned many things, young man. I have listened to my elders and I have listened to the rocks and the trees. I have learned quite a lot about camping along the lonely forest tracks too. So making a cup of tea on a miserable afternoon like this is one of my special talents," laughed The Hierophant.

Warmed by this calm and friendly man, Follin asked question after question: about the forest; the wind; the earth; and the stars. As the night deepened Follin became restless.

Noticing the youth's discomfort The Hierophant asked if there was something he wished to speak to him about. Follin looked up, and quietly began to speak of his childhood; his faults and his fears.

"If I were to say sorry for all the stupid and hurtful things I've done I'd have to live to be a hundred years old," moaned Follin staring into the fire in misery.

"My son, we all act when we wish we hadn't; and we all have failed to act when we wished we had; for we are but humble beings, not gods. Sometimes, to do good in the world, we have to put our problem on the shelf until we are ready to take it down and address it. Sometimes it is wise to seek advice from those who know better than we do. Sometimes it is wise to go within to heal the hurts others have visited upon us.

"My son, life is hard for those who have no other way, but I see that you've learned things that will make your life less of a strain than it was before. I know that you have done your best to ease the suffering of others. Trust your instincts, contemplate within your inner sanctuary, and abide by the rules you have set for yourself. Above all, follow your own path." The Hierophant's voice was like a chant and Follin soon fell into a deep sleep.

Follin dreamed: *I am back at school, nine years old, a sensitive, naive little boy. My teacher is a brute who enjoys tormenting his students. Like all bullies, he takes great pleasure in the psychological and physical torture of those who can't defend themselves. This time it's going to be quite different, I am no longer a small, defenceless child.*

I wait in his storeroom with his cane in my hand: a long, thick stick I remember so well. I stand by the door so that he won't see me. When the door opens I slam it shut, he's trapped. Up comes my cane and down it flicks, again and again. He cries like so many small boys cried under his hand for decades.

The next morning Follin woke beside the campfire with a pot of water hanging from a stick above the flames. The Hierophant sat watching him.

"Do you remember your dream, my son?" Follin looked at him,

and could tell he knew much of his childhood experiences and his dream of revenge.

"Sometimes a teacher is not honourable but a coward, someone who preys on those who cannot defend themselves. He affected you in many ways. I too am glad he is no longer in your life. But his legacy lives on inside all those who suffered from his lust for power and pleasure."

The Hierophant paused to pour them both a cup of tea, then continued. "There are many wounded souls who have felt the touch of the bully in institutions throughout the world. It is sad that my profession has helped perpetuate such misery over thousands of years. But it is in man's nature to wrestle power from others for self gain."

The Hierophant poured the tea and handed a cup to Follin, asking "So what did you learn from your bully teacher?"

"Nothing," replied Follin. "I was too afraid of him and his cane to learn anything from him."

The Hierophant patiently asked the question again. "What did that bully teach you?"

"Well, I certainly learned not to bully others" Follin replied half jokingly.

"Yes, exactly". The Hierophant leaned back, sipping his tea. "What a magnificent lesson he taught you. We learn much more from our enemies than from our friends. His gift benefits not only you, but others as well. We have one less bully thanks to him." They heard the sounds of nature awaking around them.

The Hierophant took another sip from his cup of tea and continued "The acquisition of some forms of knowledge requires rigour, dedicated practice, self-discipline, determination and long hours of study. There is also that which is learned by direct experience. That is the way of the mystic..."

The Hierophant stopped speaking to tilt his head to the side and listen to the morning chorus of the forest birds, "And now it is time to sit and enjoy the sunrise."

The Lovers
Union; love; warmth; nurture; support; choice; attraction; passion.

From <u>The Pictorial Key to the Tarot</u> A.E. Waite (1911)

"Behind the man is the Tree of Life, bearing twelve fruits, and the Tree of the Knowledge of Good and Evil is behind the woman; the serpent is twining round it. The figures suggest youth, virginity, innocence and love before it is contaminated by gross material desire. This is in all simplicity the card of human love, here exhibited as part of the way, the truth and the life. It replaces, by recourse to first principles, the old card of marriage... and the later follies which depicted man between vice and virtue."

~

Follin awoke one morning. A heavy mist lay around him and the fire was cold. The youth lit his fire and broke his fast with a bowl of warmed barley oats then stepped out onto the forest track. The mist was yet to lift so he used his mystic's walk to heighten his intuition and remain focused on the path itself – it would be too easy to become lost in the mist. Using the centred walk he stepped out slowly and gently.

Unbeknown to Follin he had entered the Sanctuary of The High Priestess Hera. The Magician and The High Priestess were waiting for him. They knew that Follin was now ready to meet with his soul partner.

Before Follin could recognise where he was The Magician and The High Priestess aligned their minds and sent Follin back to the Mystic Isle.

Follin was feeling quite disjointed. It was as though he was in another world. He did not recognise the path he was now standing on but it did feel... just right. It felt like he was back home, on the Mystic Isle. Follin knew instinctively that the path before him led to his future. It would somehow become the culmination of everything he would be working for throughout his journey.

Standing to one side of the path was a young woman. She looked to be in her mid-teens, the same age as Follin. He felt an unfamiliar warmth suffuse his being. The girl was stunning to behold. She was more beautiful than any girl he had ever seen. He was captivated, mesmerised and suddenly all thoughts of his journey fled from his mind.

Follin was afraid to approach this blonde-haired beauty. What if she didn't like him? What if she was already taken? Fortunately, she rescued him from his doubts. She beckoned him to sit with her. Shyly she handed him some of her meal. At first, they just sat and ate, but then, as though by design, they began to talk.

Suddenly Follin felt the ground give way beneath him and he was falling. Slowly his descent ceased and he saw two paths stretching before him. The paths continued side by side then converged, coming together as one. They separated and turned to merge and diverge again and again. He could see stretching out into the distance the beautiful girl and himself walking those paths, separating, coming together for a while and separating again. Fleeting images of a future life with this girl flitted through his mind. He doubted his intuition: were they just imagination fuelled by wishful thinking or were they glimpses of what would be? His urgency to join with her was overpowering, he just felt he could not live without her.

When the images faded and gave way to a profound sense of well-being, Follin knew for certain that his future was with this girl and that she would bring fulfilment and meaning to his life and he to hers.

His hands shaking nervously, Follin bravely took her hands and drew her up. Smiling into her eyes he promised to return and marry her once this journey was over. The young woman smiled as her lips kissed his cheek softly, tenderly. There was a sweet chuckle deep in her throat, she too knew that he was the one.

"What is your name?" the young woman asked.

"Follin, what's yours?"

"Eve," she announced. Eve now found the courage to ask the second most important question of her life, "Where do you live?"

"I live in the south, a village called Saoirse, it means 'be true to yourself'. It's right on the edge of the forest. When I'm finished with my journey, will you join me there, at my mother's house?"

"I might," said Eve coyly. They stood for a minute, their hands joined, staring at each other, fascinated by the discovery of the other. Their twin souls reached out and touched. At that moment the spell was broken and Follin disappeared, back to the Tarot Empire.

The Chariot

Will; morality; victory; triumph; hard work; dedication; determination; self-discipline.

From <u>The Pictorial Key to the Tarot</u> A.E. Waite (1911)

"An erect and princely figure carrying a drawn sword ... He has led captivity captive; he is conquest on all planes - in the mind, in science, in progress, in certain trials of initiation. He has thus replied to the sphinx, and it is on this account that I have accepted the variation of Éliphas Lévi; two sphinxes thus draw his chariot. He is above all things triumph in the mind."

~

Follin whistled as he walked. His mood had lifted and he was feeling buoyant and happy. He recalled experiencing a lovely day-dream, it was as though he had gone back to his Mystic Isle to meet a beautiful girl, his soul partner... or, perhaps it was real?

Continuing his journey, Follin noticed that the path now became narrow and the landscape more rugged. Obstacles appeared before him and he soon lost his joyful mood to rage impotently at every stubbed toe and every branch that whipped viciously at his face. Giving way to his frustrations he collapsed to the side of the path in bitter despair at his failure to make headway. He was distracted so much that he had forgotten his centred walking.

He struggled down to the riverbank and splashed his face. The shock of the cold water cleared his head and he began to contemplate his next move. Now he began to feel tired from pushing through the dense undergrowth. A pleasant fatigue engulfed him and he had to close his eyes. Leaning his back against a tree trunk he nodded off to sleep.

Follin was startled from his nap by the sound of horses' hooves thundering towards him. Metal wheels shedding bright sparks came crashing towards the very tree he was leaning against. Branches snapped and fell about him as two massive horses skidded to a shuddering halt. Follin noted that one was white and the other black and they were pulling a golden chariot.

Standing in the chariot, holding the reins steady as the horses plunged and snorted, was a handsome, battle-scarred warrior. He radiated an aura of personal power. Follin saw that this warrior was quite capable of bending those wild horses to his will. Judging by its condition, The Charioteer's armour had seen, and survived, many a battle. Follin noted that the armour bore no holes to mark an injury.

He was flabbergasted and overawed at the sight before him. He

Strength

Courage; willpower; flow; no expectations; non-attachment to outcomes; softness; fortitude; patience; self-control.

From The Pictorial Key to the Tarot A.E. Waite (1911)

"A woman, over whose head there broods the same symbol of life which we have seen in the card of the Magician, is closing the jaws of a lion. The only point in which this design differs from the conventional presentations is that her beneficent fortitude has already subdued the lion, which is being led by a chain of flowers… There is one aspect in which the lion signifies the passions, and she who is called Strength is the higher nature in its liberation. It has walked upon the asp and the basilisk and has trodden down the lion and the dragon."

~

Follin now wanted so much to develop his personal power and strength of arms. Unfortunately, and despite The Hierophant's wise words, he projected his desire to dominate those who had hurt him in the past. There were moments when he became arrogant and self-centred, still tempted to indulge in thoughts of ways to punish the bullies at school who hurt and humiliated him. This was a pivotal point in his life, a time when he might swing either way - to become either a good man, or a bad one. The young man knew he would now win against his former foes because he no longer feared them.

It was during such a reverie that he spied a woman. She was not large nor powerful yet she emanated an aura of Strength. Follin watched wide-eyed as she gently closed the jaws of a massive, wild lion.

Fascinated, he moved closer, the better to witness her power over the wild beast. She had tamed the raging lion with no physical effort at all. He slowly, and carefully, approached her and the now quiet beast. Follin begged her to explain how she had done the impossible. How did she apply her will to control this powerful wild animal?

"Follin, the way to achieve control over your wild urges and instincts is to use your inner strength. I did not close the lion's jaws. I was stroking him and he closed them of his own accord. My strength lies in exercising patience and having no expectations for my actions. It has taken me years of self-discipline to achieve this."

The woman looked into the youth's eyes knowing exactly what was on his mind. She saw Follin's anger and his confusion, and knew that he was struggling to apply his newfound will to control his destiny.

"Lady, what is it that I need to gain control over? Isn't it my enemies? Like those who beat me up at school?" he asked.

"The lion within sets its sights on what it wants, then races wildly forwards to satisfy its urge. With its enormous strength it allows nothing to get in its way. When we have a desire to conquer others we set ourselves on the path of domination, a path that lacks respect, it strips the will from others. This leads to a wasted life of dishonourable conquests. Even the innocent can be harmed. Control yourself, not your enemies. This is the path without guilt, remorse or regret."

They walked along the river bank until they came to a small, earthen cottage. Its roof of thatch was covered in moss and the walls were of rammed earth. All around were vegetable patches, wildflowers and grapevines climbed the cottage walls. The lion followed and lay at the lady's feet as she sat down at a wooden table. It was covered with fruits, a crock of butter, preserves and freshly baked bread. She invited Follin to sit with her and share her meal. As he did so the lion got up and moved to lie at Follin's feet.

He froze. *'I guess now is a good time to practice my inner strength,'* he thought to himself and remained seated.

She could see that Follin was perplexed so she continued: "A monk with his begging bowl sits and accepts whatever comes his way. Awaking in the morning and allowing the day to unfold with no plan. Allowing destiny to manifest without your interference. Wandering through the forest taking what each day offers... Reacting when the need arises, rather than when prompted by fear, feeling or desire. These are some of the ways to develop inner strength."

Follin was mesmerised by her and hung on every word she spoke. He was so engrossed that he even forgot to eat any of the food on the table. Before long Follin found the courage to confess his confusion.

Strength spoke again. "The wildness of the lion within us includes the forces of pride, greed, lust, jealousy and fear. For those who walk the mystic's path, taming the wild nature within us is, perhaps, the most important of all challenges and the most difficult. You need to ask yourself if you wish to control your wildness. If yes, then to continue to allow your innate animal urges free rein would be contrary to developing your willpower. Do you think that the monk with an empty begging bowl does not feel hunger? He chooses to accept the possibility that he may remain hungry yet continues to sit, unattached to the outcome."

Strength continued "It takes self-discipline to achieve the control I have demonstrated for you. Not only control of your feelings, fears and urges but your thoughts as well. It requires dedicated, sustained focus to learn to trust yourself to act spontaneously and appropriately. Therein lies self-control."

Strength poured two cups of herbal tea and nodded for Follin to partake of the food on the table. She smiled to herself when she saw how the young man carefully took only what was necessary to break his fast.

The Hermit
Solitude; deliberate isolation; meditation; inner healing; introspection; the search for truth.

From The Pictorial Key to the Tarot A.E. Waite (1911)

"I have said that this is a card of attainment, and to extend this conception the figure is seen holding up his beacon on an eminence... His beacon intimates that "where I am, you also may be." It is further a card which is understood quite incorrectly when it is connected with the idea of occult isolation, as the protection of personal magnetism against admixture."

~

Follin missed his father. During his times of meditation and walking at night he would recall how the two would go camping in the forest. He was now certain that his father sought these times of solitude and seclusion to practise special forms of meditation. His father had once told him that mystics used prayer, contemplation and meditation as a path to enlightenment. Back then his father's words made little sense to Follin; he was more interested in the chestnuts roasting in the fire. It was the closeness of these times together that Follin missed so much now.

One night Follin remembered his father telling him how he used his dreams on his own mystic's path. His father called it 'deliberate dreaming' and explained that it was another way to use the time of sleeping. Follin followed his father's half-remembered instructions. As a result of using his father's technique he came upon extraordinary wonders on his wanderings among the stars at night.

Follin felt that no one would believe him if he told them how he left his body at night to explore the marvels of the universe or crossed dimensions between the astral planes. He found that the solitude of the hermitage made his mystic studies so much easier.

One day he was startled by the sound of a child sobbing. He searched all around the cottage but could find no child. The sobbing continued. It caused a painful sadness, a loneliness deep within his chest. Follin closed his eyes and went within his psyche to find the source of this sadness. There he found a memory of himself as a child, hurt and lonely, crying in his bedroom. He stepped into this memory appearing as a young man to this small, inner child. He hugged his inner child to his chest and said, *'It wasn't your fault, you didn't make him go away, you were just a child. You did nothing to cause him to leave.'*

Follin found that hugging his inner child made his heart quiet and his soul at peace. The grief he felt when his father, the Mage of

Saoirse, left after his older brother died of the plague, was now something he could continue to process in his daily meditations.

With time and meditation, the ache of grief in his chest slowly disappeared. He then knew it was time to leave the sanctuary of his moss covered Hermitage.

In preparation for his departure, Follin gathered and chopped enough wood to fill the lean-to, cleaned the inside of the cottage as best he could, chose enough of the preserved food to last him a few days and packed his belongings. On the table outside he left his last gifts of food for his unknown benefactor and two words scrawled on bark with the burnt end of a pointed stick. *Thankyou Goodbye.*

In some ways Follin felt he was back at the start of his journey, back to being a young fool full of wonder and raw potential, acknowledging his past and eager for his future. His journey had led him to this period of solitude and exploration within, and, having embarked on the internal journey to heal his body and spirit, he found it time to move on. He now yearned for new challenges, so he resumed his Fool's journey.

Wheel of Fortune

What goes up must come down; reap what you sow; destiny; fate; karma; luck of the draw; chance; a gamble; that's life.

From The Pictorial Key to the Tarot A.E. Waite (1911)

"...the symbolic picture stands for the perpetual motion of a fluidic universe and for the flux of human life."

~

Follin soon came across a vibrant, bustling village. He looked at the riches of the villagers, their neat houses and the beautiful clothing they wore. *'Perhaps I can find some work here and buy myself some new clothes and shoes?'* Follin hoped that the Wheel of Fortune would turn and lift his spirits upwards.

A tavern keeper gave him work in his kitchen washing dishes and serving the customers. It was hard work for little pay. On the upside, he was given three meals each day and a bed in a corner, shared with three others. Follin worked hard and soon found that people appreciated his quick smile and eagerness to help when the tavern was busy.

With his scant wages, he bought himself the best shoes he could afford. To a wanderer, such as Follin had become, shoes were his most precious possession. Many a time he had to stuff dry grass into the soles of his shoes to stop the sharp stones bruising his feet, or to keep his feet warm. On other occasions, he would walk barefooted on soft, grassy tracks to save his shoe leather.

Clothing and other accessories were often left in the rooms by travellers. When the tavern keeper saw how well Follin worked, he gave him a used pair of trousers, a shirt and a jacket to wear while working. When Follin had earned enough to buy his own clothes he went out and bought a sturdy cloak to keep the rain off for when he was back on his journey through the forests of the Tarot Empire.

But bad times often follow good and one day Follin was accused of stealing money from a customer's purse. The man and his cronies dragged him before the tavern keeper.

Not wishing to lose any of his regular, big-spending customers, the tavern keeper chose to blame the innocent Follin. He sent one of the girls who worked behind the bar to collect Follin's belongings, then he physically threw him down the tavern stairs into the dusty street. The tavern keeper took Follin's sturdy new boots and waterproof cloak and handed them to the complaining customer to make amends.

Luckily Follin had hidden The Magician's four gifts and the scrolls beneath his old, tattered clothing in the, by now, very dirty bundle on his staff. He briefly thought of using the Coin to buy back his cloak and boots but instinctively knew that it would not be honouring the gift to do so.

It was a bitter lesson on injustice that Follin struggled to understand. As he picked up his few remaining belongings from the dirty street he felt an intense surge of outrage. Spying the hilt of The Magician's dagger protruding from his bundle he grabbed it and started back up the stairs.

As Follin shifted his grip to throw his dagger at the tavern keeper's retreating back he heard Strength's voice. The image of a raging lion racing towards its prey was superimposed on the image of the lion resting at his feet. In that split second Follin applied his self-control and chose dominion over himself rather than give in to the urge for revenge. He turned back down the steps, thrust the dagger into his belt, picked up his belongings and started back on the dirt track, just as he had done so many times before.

One of the boys who worked with Follin, and respected him and his hard work, had watched the wretched youth thrown from the tavern with horror. Careful not to be seen by the owner he caught up with his friend as he was walking out of the town.

"Follin," he called, "don't despair, we're all destined to follow the wheel of life. In bad times we may find ourselves on our way up towards happiness and success. But even though we may be on top, it mightn't last, the Wheel of Fortune can easily turn and send us back down to misery again."

Follin paused and turned to his friend, "I was so happy there,

Jackson. I worked hard and thought everyone liked me. You were all so nice to me. I was making money, too, and that meant I could buy what I needed and even some small things that took my fancy. Why is it that when things seem so good, suddenly they can come crashing down around our ears?"

"I'm sorry, Follin, I wish the tavern master had some morals and the courage to stand up to those bullies. They've done this before. But I must run and get back to work." As he turned Jackson called over his shoulder, "My dad always said that a successful person forges his own destiny. Don't let the Wheel of Fortune roll over and squash you again, Follin!"

In a state of depression, and no little pain, Follin shouldered his meagre belongings, his scrolls and gifts wrapped in dirty laundry, and his staff, then took to wandering the forest paths once again. He never learned who stole the money, if anyone indeed had; or whether it was jealousy that drove someone to accuse him of the theft.

~

Follin shrugged his shoulders as he resumed his journey. Inside his head he heard, *'such is life'*. All he could think of was how he was back on the road with nothing to show for all his hard work, or so it seemed.

Justice
Fairness; balance; wisdom; examination; decisions; weighing up advice; negotiation; compromise; law; legal system.

From <u>The Pictorial Key to the Tarot</u> A.E. Waite (1911)

"It will be seen, ... that the figure is seated between pillars, like the High Priestess, and on this account it seems desirable to indicate that the moral principle which deals unto every man according to his works - while, of course, it is in strict analogy with higher things; - differs in its essence from the spiritual justice which is involved in the idea of election... It is analogous to the possession of the faerie gifts and the high gifts and the gracious gifts of the poet: we have them or have not, and their presence is as much a mystery as their absence... In conclusion, the pillars of Justice open into one world and the pillars of the High Priestess into another."

~

Follin felt miserable at his misfortune and wandered aimlessly. His pack still contained the gifts he was given by The Magician, and The High Priestess' scrolls were now well worn, the stiff paper beginning to crack from use. Over the days and weeks, his path slowly became a little clearer and a little easier to follow.

One day as Follin bent down to drink from a stream he remembered The Magician's cup. He unwrapped it, thinking to use it to scoop up the water. Just as he did so he remembered a story his father had told him.

'I was sitting in tavern with a businessman from a neighbouring town and we paused our discussion to share a pipe or two. The businessman couldn't be bothered walking over to the fire to light a taper. "Here, famous mage, use your wand to light my pipe, will you." I knew then not to enter into business with him as he showed that he was irresponsible, a wastrel.'

Follin gently rewrapped The Magician's cup and used his cupped hands to drink from the stream.

As he approached another village, Follin came across a stern looking woman. From her apparel it appeared that she was a woman of Justice. She was sitting beside a river crossing. Her cloak was emblazoned with a sword on one side, and a set of scales on the other. He saw that she was adjudicating a conflict between two men. The men soon nodded to her and then to each other. They shook hands and left, heading in opposite directions.

The stern faced woman looked up from gathering her law books, to see Follin watching. She invited him to sit beside her. Follin looked into her blue, unblinking eyes as she asked him about his travels. Follin found that, despite trying his best to remain calm, he could not control his mind or his voice.

Follin told Justice about the tavern incident. She listened to his tale carefully, examining both sides and asking for more detail on certain aspects.

"As the Wheel of Fortune turns, one needs to accept one's fate with humility and good humour, even when unjustly accused with no possibility of redress."

Justice then held out both her hands, palms facing to the sky. One hand filled with coins. She then lifted the other, like a set of scales; this hand seemed to hold a dull light. Her hand tilted and half the coins fell to the ground, disintegrating on impact. This time the light in the other hand started to grow brighter and began to drop. They were now level, equal and balanced. Justice smiled at Follin.

"The mystic's path to enlightenment involves dedication to your purpose and the application of wisdom; these must always remain in balance. To survive this journey you need to give a little, and take a little. Sometimes we are placed in situations where we must negotiate and compromise, balancing our needs with the needs of others. As my old friend the beekeeper always reminds me, nectar is better than vinegar if you want to attract bees."

Follin nodded, though he was not sure he understood.

"To walk the path of enlightenment the mystic needs to live a virtuous life. However, sometimes the mystic needs to take a stand and be prepared to defend it," she said. "I don't mean that one must fight, like the two men I spoke to when you saw me. What I mean, Follin, is that sometimes a mystic must hold to what he or she believes to be true and honourable."

Follin realised that he had spent the past weeks focused on trying to resolve his resentment of being thrown from the tavern and his desire for material gain. It was as Justice had said: he had focused on taking, rather than giving. 'Giving' was easy for the Mystic Isle youth, but when he needed money for his boots and cloak he became solely focused on 'taking'. He wanted to make as much money as he could so that he might afford new apparel for his journey. While working at the tavern he had not been seeking internal balance at all.

In this wise woman's voice, he heard an echo of The Empress, The Emperor, The Hierophant, Mage Hermes and The High Priestess Hera. Follin realised that the knowledge imparted by Justice built on his earlier lessons and shed light on his recent experiences.

Follin left the lady of Justice with his head filled with jumbled thoughts. He remembered his lessons with The Empress and decided he needed to ground himself and release this mental confusion physically by using the centred walk she had taught him. He knew that her walking exercise would help foster his personal power and calm his mind. Deliberately he pointed his toes forward on the forested path to walk softly and gently.

The Hanged Man

Reversal; sacrifice; punishment; introspection; meditation; different perspective; new ideas; time out; a different approach; solutions by alternate means.

From <u>The Pictorial Key to the Tarot</u> A.E. Waite (1911)

"It should be noted (1) that the tree of sacrifice is living wood, with leaves thereon; (2) that the face expresses deep entrancement, not suffering; (3) that the figure, as a whole, suggests life in suspension, but life and not death. It is a card of profound significance, but all the significance is veiled... It has been called falsely a card of martyrdom, a card of prudence, a card of the Great Work, a card of duty... He who can understand that the story of his higher nature is imbedded in this symbolism will receive intimations concerning a great awakening that is possible, and will know that after the sacred Mystery of Death there is a glorious Mystery of Resurrection."

~

Follin now knew that he desperately needed to find a new perspective to his life. He felt his former foundations, the meaningfulness of his existence, had been shattered by the events at the tavern. Despite his encounter with Justice, he still felt the shame and injustice of being so harshly punished for a crime he had not committed.

On the side of his path now appeared a large, leafy oak tree whose roots and trunk had pushed apart the earth around it. Standing beneath this tree and looking up, he could barely see the sky through its thick, green canopy.

It was early afternoon and Follin began to relax as he stared upwards towards the heavens. As he did so he felt an overwhelming fatigue in his limbs and collapsed against the tree trunk. Then he began to grow restless. He intuited that he needed a novel way to look within himself, to find how he might apply the lessons Justice had imparted.

He sat; he wriggled; he lay down on his stomach; then on his back; but it was no use. Follin just could not get comfortable nor could he focus his mind the way he wanted to. Finally he relaxed in a position that seemed just right – it was the posture of The Hanged Man.

This time of reflection showed him a new way of looking at problems. Insights came to him in connection with issues he that had plagued him for years. Then it came to him: meditation and contemplation required flexibility, sometimes a novel technique could reveal answers to difficult queries. Sometimes sacrificing the comfort of beliefs or habits is necessary to arrive at a new perspective.

The Hanged Man posture opened up new ways for him to explore his inner and outer world issues. He recalled The Hierophant's lesson about enemies being our best teachers. While his sense of injustice remained, he now better understood Justice's message, though he knew his understanding remained incomplete.

Follin also realised that learning about something was not enough. Learning how to meditate was insufficient, he needed to practise every day. Then he thought of the myriad other lessons from his teachers. *'If I practised daily everything they have taught me I'd never leave my campfire.'*

He heard The Magician's voice *'selfless dedicated effort'*.

From The High Priestess Hera came a whisper *'trust your intuition ...stillness... solitude... silence... meditation... dreaming'*

Remembering the The Empress he heard *'inner balance ... harmony ... personal power ...centred walking ...softly, gently...'*

The Emperor's voice was clear in his mind *'set your boundaries and be prepared to defend them ... delegation ... negotiation... rule yourself for the good of others'*

The Hierophant's words echoed in his mind *'abide by the rules you have set for yourself ...we learn from our enemies'*

He recalled Sir Darwyn, The Charioteer's laughter sounded in Follin's mind as he said *'determination ... self-discipline ... the will to control your own fate ... let nothing sway you from your purpose ... accept nothing but your best'*

Strength's words flowed as he saw an image of the lion resting at her feet *'self-control...no expectations...patience'*.

Follin realised, as if ticking items on a list, that he had in fact been practising much of what he had been taught as he walked through the forest each day. He regularly used The Empress' centred walking, when he remembered and was not distracted, and practised his nightly meditations. It was the interaction with other humans that he needed, to practise his self-control and to learn from his enemies, as he had done at the tavern. To do so alone in the forest was easy...

When he opened his eyes he found himself upside down,

hanging by his feet, held firm by a thick branch. His belongings lay scattered on the ground beneath him. Follin did not even care, he felt wonderfully refreshed.

Follin knew he could not stay this way, he needed to move on. This experience of The Hanged Man had filled him with energy and inspiration. With a chuckle, he righted himself, freed his feet, jumped down from the tree, packed his belongings, including the dagger that had slipped from his waist, and continued on, into the sun-dappled forest.

Death

Endings; beginnings; reincarnation; acceptance of the inevitability of change; new opportunities after disappointment or loss; grief and loss; reality; down-to-earth outcomes; eliminating non-essentials.

From <u>The Pictorial Key to the Tarot</u> A.E. Waite (1911)

"The veil or mask of life is perpetuated in change, transformation and passage from lower to higher... the Mystic Rose, which signifies life... The natural transit of man to the next stage of his being either is or may be one form of his progress, but the exotic and almost unknown entrance, while still in this life, into the state of mystical death is a change in the form of consciousness and the passage into a state to which ordinary death is neither the path nor gate. The existing occult explanations of the 13th card are, on the whole, better than usual, rebirth, creation, destination, renewal, and the rest."

~

Over several days there developed a deep sense of dread in the forest. Although there were no leaves on the trees Follin could no longer see the sky. A thick, cloying mist grew as he walked deeper among the decaying, skeletal trees. Through the mist he could just make out a figure in the distance. It was someone riding a horse, the diffuse light of the morning sun behind him. Follin, with his new found strength of will, centred and edged cautiously closer. He was shocked to see that it was a skeleton in a black suit of armour. Only in his worst nightmares had he seen anything like this one.

Death looked intently into Follin's eyes and at that moment Follin realised that his old life was ended. He could not go back to undo the mistakes of his past nor bring back the things and people he had lost. As he recognised this truth an immense sense of dread filled his being.

Death leaned from his horse and reached out his hand. One skeletal finger lifted Follin's quaking chin so that he had to look directly into Death's eyes.

Follin heard a voice inside his head, it was the voice of Death. Follin closed his eyes and saw a succession of images as Death began to chant: *'A universe born stars form galaxies spin collide stars shine brightly die supernovae explode Sol ignites earth forms spins night day we shine die a thousand deaths in a lifetime love flames dies daylight brings life hope moonlight dreams a foreboding of endless night what dies lives what lives dies.'*

Follin forced himself to pull away from Death's vile grip. When he did he was amazed to see just an old man on a skinny horse. Compared with the immensity he had just seen, what was there to fear now?

In Death's imagery Follin saw that life was a series of cycles within cycles; they all led from endings to new beginnings. To move forward one must leave something behind. *'What goes around comes around'* he recalled The Empress saying.

The Death rider looked down at the youth, his jaw moved as though he were speaking but his voice was once more inside Follin's head. "Remember that existence is a series of cycles of birth, death and rebirth. This is also the cycle of reincarnation. Sometimes I am called to terminate a dead end project, a useless relationship, or to end a person's emotional episode of grief or sadness. Sometimes an ending is a great relief, especially to someone who is suffering. That suffering could be a failing romance, a one-way friendship, an illness or a failed business relationship. Embrace Death, do not fear it."

Follin was sure he had heard The Empress mention that Death was a reminder that nothing stays the same. It initiates change, a transformation; like the caterpillar transforming into a butterfly after a period of stasis.

Death released the youth's mind and continued on his own journey, gathering his crop of newly dead, to be recycled back to new beginnings. The morning brightened as the sun appeared out of the gloom. Follin, however, remained somewhat disturbed. The stench of Death still lingered in and around him. He needed cleansing, a healing, to clear his mind and his heart. He was in need of a new beginning of his own.

Temperance

Avoid excess; moderation; purity; wisdom; tempering creativity with the rational and the rational with the imaginal.

From <u>The Pictorial Key to the Tarot</u> A.E. Waite (1911)

"A winged angel, with the sign of the sun upon his forehead and on his breast the square and triangle of the septenary....but the figure is neither male nor female. It is held to be pouring the essences of life from chalice to chalice. It has one foot upon the earth and one upon waters, thus illustrating the nature of the essences... It is called Temperance fantastically, because, when the rule of it obtains in our consciousness, it tempers, combines and harmonises the psychic and material natures. Under that rule we know in our rational part something of whence we came and whither we are going."

~

As Follin set camp beside a large lake he saw the Angel Temperance standing at the water's edge. He sat in fascination as he watched her mixing two incompatible liquids, defying the laws of logic and rationality. He thought to himself, *'this is pure alchemy.'*

The Angel called for the young man to join her. She explained that in order to complete his journey Follin would need to exercise his will to control the power of creativity within himself.

"What I am doing now is mixing the concrete logic of the rational mind, with the inner world of the imagination; of dreams and intuition. I saw that you had a foot in each of these realms, which is why you could see me. You understood what I was doing, intuitively," she said.

Follin invited the Angel to join him at his campfire. They sat comfortably talking over their evening meal beside the cheery, crackling fire. He rarely had company on his travels along the lonely forest paths. Recognising that his meeting with the Angel was part of his journey he relaxed and enjoyed the warmth of her presence.

"Kind Angel, I've travelled the paths of this land to find peace and harmony for my troubled soul. There have been many teachers on my way who have helped, but I remain unsure of myself. I still doubt my own experiences and I don't think I can ever create balance and harmony as effortlessly as you."

Follin's hands rose to embrace his drawn face, "This place, this Tarot Empire has the most magical beings, but I am just a human. I can't do what they all want me to do, despite my daily practice. I thought I could, hanging from the tree, but now I feel so overwhelmed that sometimes I want to cry."

The Angel lifted her cup of tea and smiled at Follin. "Young man," she said with touching gentleness. "You have experienced much since you left your village. You have sat at the feet of many wise teachers, yet you still doubt your worthiness to walk this path. I know what efforts you have made to find peace within. I have watched you wipe the sweat from your brow as you purposefully strode up each soul-crushing hill on your path; I have witnessed your inner child smile with joy as you hugged him; I have walked with you in your astral dreams to show you the mysteries of the stars; I have led you by the hand when you have wandered off your path. I know you to be pure of spirit, for you have learned moderation and have tempered your soul for goodness. Listen to your instincts, go gently, go softly. Remember to temper the Divine with the mundane for, as above, so below."

'Must there be temperance in all things?' he wanted to ask. *'Are there some times when temperance is not appropriate?'* but Temperance had gone. He heard the Angel's voice as if from afar "...and with intention temper your innate urges and desires, your natural instincts to indulge in earthly pleasures..."

As Follin sat beside the fire that evening to carefully ponder her words he fell asleep, so tired that he did not even crawl into his blankets.

The Devil

Temptation; bondage; greed; lust; blind desire; blind ignorance; material desires; self-control; opportunity to move after stagnation; transformation; evolution; insight; choice; knowledge; wisdom earned.

From <u>The Pictorial Key to the Tarot</u> A.E. Waite (1911)

"The Horned Goat of Mendes… There is a ring in front of the altar, from which two chains are carried to the necks of two figures, male and female... Hereof is the chain and fatality of the material life. The figures are tailed, to signify the animal nature, but there is human intelligence in the faces, and he who is exalted above them is not to be their master for ever. Even now, he is also a bondsman, sustained by the evil that is in him and blind to the liberty of service... What it does signify is the Dweller on the Threshold..."

~

Several nights later, Follin awoke inside a dream. He found himself walking with the Angel Temperance on a grassy hill. There was something familiar about the man riding towards him. It was The Emperor. He leapt from his horse and hugged the young man with great warmth.

"I see that you have found another beautiful lady to advise you. I think, from the company you keep, that you will have a very important encounter tonight. Go gently, go softly, son, and do not forget to consider your options and then vigorously defend your boundaries."

The Angel then swept Follin into the air. Together they flew through the sky to alight at the mouth of a cave resting at the base of a cloud swept peak. Although Follin did not know it, he was now in the Hindamar Mountains in the northern Tarot Empire.

The cave was deep and dark and Follin could smell the mustiness of mildew. As he peered inside he saw a Devil-like man walking towards them. Follin blinked. *'No it can't be,'* he thought. *'He looks like he is half goat and half man?'*

The Devil figure introduced himself, "Welcome to Pluto's Cave. With the help of my friend, the Angel Temperance, you have crossed the threshold of consciousness and have entered my realm, the Underworld. But understand, once you enter my realm you will not return to the world unchanged." Follin gulped audibly.

"I am Pluto, but some call me Hades, Lord of the Underworld; or Pan, the God of the Earth, of nature and the seasons. I appear to many people in many guises, as a single, dual or multiple entity. To some I appear as the Capricorn sea goat. To those with greed or great fear in their hearts, I sometimes choose to appear as Satan, the tempter of prophets, priests and others."

The god Pan smiled, then laughed loudly, "For at least ten

thousand years humanity has tended goats for their hides, milk, meat and everything else they could take from them, and yet in that form I am cast as The Devil. Maybe it is my human half they fear so much?" Follin felt a combination of sadness, irony and a desire to laugh with this funny, humanlike god.

"I prefer to appear to you now in my favourite form, Pan."

Follin's eyes were fixated on the goat-god. "What do you actually do, God Pan?" he asked in awe.

Pan, the god of the seasons, and of life itself, replied, "I give humanity certain lessons in life. I provide them with opportunities to test their spiritual resolve." Pan smiled, he could read Follin's mind as the young man looked around him. "I can see that you judge me by my filthy cave. Yet it is also magnificent! Walk with me, and you will see that all you could ever desire lies within."

Together the three entered an immense cavern. Laid out before them was indeed everything a young man could desire. Wealth, sex, power, love, greed, gluttony... each shimmering object reflected a sin, sins that hinder humanity's path to enlightenment.

"Please," offered Pan, "take anything you wish, anything. You might need something later."

Pan smiled and yet a tear broke free from the corner of his eye to fall to the cavern floor. Follin was so struck with lust and greed at the possibilities before him, that he did not notice.

"Why, thank you, yes. I think I do need some gold to help me get back home, and new boots and a cloak..." The Mystic Isle youth looked with wonder and desire at all the objects available, all within his grasp. All he had to do was reach out and grab them.

"I'm going back home soon, to be with my Lover, Eve. She's probably already waiting for me, you know. I could take enough gold for when we have a family. Families are expensive... and I need to bring her a gift... maybe she would like this... no, no, maybe that..."

Suddenly snatching his hand back from the many temptations before him, Follin's scream echoed against the cavern walls.

"NO! NO! NO! You tricked me! I know what you're doing! Let me be gone from this place, Angel, please!" Follin gasped.

"Ah" said The Devil God Pan Hades Pluto. "You have remembered the story of the temptation of the Exalted One during her time in the wilderness. I offered her the world, but she remained steadfast. Your path to enlightenment is very much the same path adepts have walked before you. Some failed and some succeeded, as you have. Mystics strive hard not to submit to the temptations of the material world, their goal is to recognise their boundaries and to remain virtuous in all things. Mystics try to hold true to their path seeking to conquer temptation at every level of their being: physical, mental, material, emotional and spiritual."

Suppressing a desire to ask for a notebook and pencil so that he could write these words down to study later, Follin calmed himself and stood politely before Pan. With his head bowed, he reached out to grasp the god's hand in his own.

"I am so sorry for judging you, Lord. Your gift is the most precious of all. I know that I have so much more to learn. I will find a suitable gift of my own making for my beloved. Thank you for this valuable lesson in humility and temperance. Thank you with all my heart."

Throughout the time he was in the cave, Follin had not noticed two naked figures bound in chains. He did now. They seemed calm and, on closer inspection, he saw that the chains around their ankles were but loosely shackled to the cavern floor. They could easily set themselves free if they wished. He realised that they were chained by their lust, prisoners of their own greed.

"One last thing, young Fool, though I don't think we can call you a fool for much longer," smiled Pan. "I have something for you, something that you will always remember of your visit to my cave. If you would, please enter a light trance and meld with me. My real gift is even greater than you could have ever gained from this storehouse of precious nothings."

Follin closed his eyes. Feeling with his mind he flowed gently into Pan's body. It was more a force drawing him, pulling his mind into the god's body. Then, with a sudden shock, Follin felt incredibly alive. His eyes shot open, he could see in the dark! He ran outside the cave and then into the deep forest of the Hindamar Mountains. He could feel the earth's heartbeat; the mountain's breath; the animals and plants spoke to him; his senses soared with joy.

'Oh my, I can sense what ailments each plant can heal. I can sense their life force. I see the swirls of energy around them. I feel their character and I can taste their purpose. I now understand why the cycles of life go round and round, cycles within cycles...' Follin looked at his feet. They were the feet of a goat, Pan's feet.

There now came a pull from the cave. "Oh please dear Angel, let me stay for a while longer, I want to feel like this forever!" pleaded the youth.

"Follin, alas, you are not a god and I cannot let you stay any longer," said Temperance standing beside Pan. "You have passed the tests we gave you. Thank you, Pan, my friend, but we must go now. This young man has only a short rest before he must wake."

The Angel picked up the now sleeping youth in her arms and deposited him on his grassy bed beside the lake. The sun was just rising but she let him sleep a little longer.

Follin finally woke to the light of the sun shining on his face. It felt like he had just lived an entire lifetime. He marvelled at his strange dream. *'No, that was not a dream. I was there, in Pan the goat-god's body. I felt the plants' healing auras, the energy of the mountains and the earth itself. I was there in Pan's Underworld too.*

He gave me such an incredible gift, I wonder if I will ever again feel such a joy like that again.'

Later that day as Follin wandered through the forest, his memory of his time with Pan began to fade and his thoughts turned to Eve. *'Maybe I should have accepted something for her'* then *'No, that was part of Pan's temptation, that I thought it was all right to take something for another, when in doing so it was to see the pleasure in her eyes at receiving such a valuable object. No, when I give Eve a gift it must be of my own making...for her and her alone, without expectation of gratitude or reward...'*

Follin then recalled his brief meeting with The Emperor. *'He said that I should remember to recognise and then vigorously defend my boundaries. That must be the boundary of knowing right from wrong, not to allow someone else to tempt me to make the wrong decision. I suppose that's something like he has to do when he has to make an important decision on how to rule his Empire.'*

That night, and every night thereafter, as Follin sat quietly in the comfort of his blazing fire, he selected a small branch. He placed the tip against his heart and, when he felt it ignite, tenderly laid it on the fire. As the sparks flew up into the sky they took with them Follin's fond wishes for Eve's well-being.

The Tower

Dramatic and sudden change; unprepared; opportunity; breaking down outdated structures or beliefs; new beginnings after the old order has been destroyed.

From <u>The Pictorial Key to the Tarot</u> A.E. Waite (1911)

"Occult explanations attached to this card are meagre... I agree... that it is the ruin of the House of We, when evil has prevailed therein, and above all that it is the rending of a House of Doctrine. I understand that the reference is, however, to a House of Falsehood. It illustrates also in the most comprehensive way the old truth that "except the Lord build the house, they labour in vain that build it."... The Tower has been spoken of as the chastisement of pride and the intellect overwhelmed in the attempt to penetrate the Mystery of God; but in neither case do these explanations account for the two persons who are the living sufferers."

~

As Follin sat by his campfire enjoying his morning porridge of barley oats, mushrooms and wild greens, he noticed a stone Tower in the distance. It was massive and so tall it touched the sky. A feeling of déjà vu took hold of him. Its familiarity astounded him; he saw vague visions in his head of buildings, blueprints, structures and cathedrals though he had never seen them previously.

Follin recognised that such a robust structure was something that would last forever, it could never be destroyed. Yet, suddenly, a bolt of lightning struck The Tower from a clear, cloudless sky. Its crowned parapet was shattered into many pieces, the stones supporting it crashed to the ground with a roar. Clouds of dust billowed around its base.

Quickly sitting up straight Follin thought *'What on earth just happened?'* After the wonderful experience of being in Pan's body, this seemed completely unreal and wrong. Turning his mind to consider the tragedy from a spiritual perspective, Follin understood that sometimes what we think is real, is not.

That made him think of his encounter with Death, and how Death had said that some things end to make way for new beginnings. Sometimes what we consider solid is weak and what we think will remain true forever may not remain true tomorrow. What we consider unchanging must give way to the inevitability of transformation.

'This Tower looked like it would stand forever. But like almost every belief I had in childhood, it has fallen.' Follin continued to ponder the situation before him. *'I need to contemplate the mystery of 'change'. I'll use The Hanged Man technique for this, I think.'*

Follin lay on his back then flipped his legs into the air supporting his body on his shoulders and hands. He was now in an upside-down position. Although it was uncomfortable, when he opened his eyes he saw the world in a different way. Closing his eyes once more he slowly returned to his normal meditation posture. He now lay on his back but his visual perspective was still upside-down.

Maintaining this convoluted visual perspective was difficult. Fortunately, Follin had been avidly practising this method to change his perspective, so he continued until his mind released its hold and he floated out of his body.

Two figures had fallen from The Tower. He had not noticed them before, but now that he was on the astral plane Follin could clearly see them, confused and disturbed.

"What happened?" asked one of them, a woman, trembling in shock. She looked around trying to make sense of the shattered Tower below her.

"I don't know," replied her male co-worker who was just as confused and in much the same condition. "We were watching the sky waiting for clouds to come, and then we were falling. I wonder, are we dead?" he asked the woman floating beside him. With some frustration he continued, "I knew this damn tower was weakened by rising damp and would collapse one day. I told the authorities it needed to be pulled down and replaced with a more solid structure. I told them, I did, now look at it, just a pile of rubble."

"Hello," Follin introduced himself. "I hope I can help you. I saw your Tower struck by lightning and collapse. As you said, sir, you must both be dead because I don't meet many people who aren't either dead or archetypes, on this plane of existence."

"Oh, damn, I had so much to do too. Now I'll have to start all over again," cried the woman in frustration.

"Dead? I thought so, it certainly explains why we're floating above that pile of rubble below us." The man put his hand to his chin and thought for a moment. "I'd like to go and see my family, that's what I want to do. I want to go to them and say goodbye. I know I'll be fine, I've learned that we all go to heaven when we die, so I'll say goodbye then head off to find this 'heaven' place." He looked at the woman who was still complaining about her loss. The man then turned to Follin and thanked him and promptly disappeared.

Follin was now left with the woman. "Madam, if I can help, please just ask."

"Help? What, help me to finish my sky-gazing? Please just leave me be. I wasn't prepared for this interruption. I need to get back to my work as quick as possible. I didn't come to work on my Rest Day for this to happen. I may as well have stayed at home with my husband and children. They begged me to go with them on a picnic instead of going to work today..." Just then her face brightened. "Well, I don't believe it! That's my mother and grandmother there, can you see them? They've come to take me home." The woman waved to Follin as she excitedly moved off to join her astral family.

When Follin returned to his body and wakefulness, he immediately reached for his journal.

The blasted Tower was so shocking that it had upset Follin's internal balance. His meditation in such a strange posture, upside-down, demonstrated both the shocking nature of change, and that sometimes even an experienced mystic needs to try something different to find the answers he or she seeks.

Follin wrote that sometimes change was dramatic, like a lightning bolt. Sometimes a dramatic change is necessary for new and more beautiful things to be built in its place. Change, as Death had told him, heralds new growth.

The Tower represented a human construct that had outlived its usefulness - it needed to be replaced. Follin considered that each of those people had unfinished business that they had failed to attend to. Their lives remained fixated on their work, not on their spiritual needs. Their destiny was sealed when The Tower was struck by lightning. Each had the opportunity to take the day off to be with family, but they had ignored their other needs and stayed at work.

Follin was reminded of a Mystic Isle legend about a tower that was built by humans to climb to the heavens, to bypass the mystic's path of hardship, labour and virtuous living. One of the gods destroyed the tower as a warning to all that enlightenment, or entry into Heaven, must be earned. It also illustrated that change can strike at any time, without warning – just like a lightning bolt from a clear sky.

'The suddenness reminds us to practice our daily mystical exercises and meditations. We endeavour to consider and fulfil each of our needs, knowing that at any time we too may be blasted into nothingness, without warning' he wrote in his journal.

To Follin the two sky-gazers represented those who were not prepared for their lives to change. He also realised that remaining too long in a job, a relationship, or a mindset, may be fatal.

'Not necessarily mortally fatal, but the relationship may fail before you are ready for it; the job may end before you have found one to replace it; the mindset you had may be shattered, forcing you to challenge the beliefs you had held so close,' he wrote. *'Wow'*, he thought as he reread his notes, *'when did I get so wise?'*

Follin realised that preparation for change and developing the flexibility and adaptability to manage it, are essential components of the mystic's daily practice. Each evening he reminded himself to examine what he may have left undone, *'If I died tonight what would I regret?'*

The Star

Hope; blessings; faith; inner strength; help is on its way; guidance.

From <u>The Pictorial Key to the Tarot</u> A.E. Waite (1911)

"She pours Water of Life from two great ewers, irrigating sea and land. Behind her is rising ground and on the right a shrub or tree, whereon a bird alights. The figure expresses eternal youth and beauty....That which the figure communicates to the living scene is the substance of the heavens and the elements. It has been said truly that the mottoes of this card are "Waters of Life freely" and "Gifts of the Spirit."

~

One day the forest stopped abruptly, giving way to the sea. Follin had experienced a dramatic change within himself over the past months. He could now understand the positive and negative sides of misfortune. He began to experience a profound confidence in his own spiritual growth but he knew that he still needed hope and guidance.

Night had fallen as he sat by his campfire on a beach at the forest's edge. Follin pondered The Tower mystery. *'Would I be prepared if my world was shattered by an event as dramatic as that?'* he asked himself.

As Follin relaxed and sipped his cup of tea, he noticed, up in the star filled night sky, a very bright Star, that grew until it was bigger and brighter than a rising full moon. Its white light reflected on the sea shimmered black and silver into the distance like a stairway rising to heaven

Near him, at the start of that silvery beam, there appeared a beautiful woman tending a garden on the edge of the forest. She was bathed in light, radiant, the embodiment of The Star above her. The woman seemed to be completely engrossed in her gardening.

In each hand she held a cup; one watering the garden, the other poured water into the sea. He walked closer so that he could see what she was doing. The woman smiled and offered him a drink from one of the cups. A soft warmth flowed through him. She then offered Follin fruit from her garden. Biting into the fruit Follin felt a jolt of energy in his body, it burned as though a fire had been lit within him.

"Star Lady, I've felt this magical, alive feeling before, when I met The Empress. She must have done something to me because I couldn't sleep the night I first met her. Is this the same energy?" he asked.

"The Empress represents fertility, and her aura assists the mystic in raising his or her own energy. The mystic's journey is extremely demanding. It is at this stage that most begin to flounder, many give up. As you approach the goal of your journey you need a boost of energy to assist you in reaching that goal. My gift will help you," The Star replied.

"Whenever in doubt, look up and follow The Star, it will always guide you to safety." Her pure, inner glow and gentle compassion filled Follin with a bright hope.

"Lady of The Star, I see you are happy and contented working your garden, but you have no clothes, aren't you cold? Would you like to borrow my woollen coat to keep warm?" Follin asked politely.

She giggled lightly, "Follin, you are such a gentleman. I am warmed by my happiness, and my nakedness demonstrates to you that I am honourable and trustworthy – I have nothing to hide."

Follin's face blushed a bright red, "Yes, I can see you've nothing to hide. You're really beautiful." He caught himself before he said anything to embarrass himself. Then he realised he was staring at her.

Again the naked Starwoman giggled, fully aware of the impact her image had on the young man. "Follin, I am not human, this is a form I can take when I choose to. I sometimes adopt this form to hold the mystic's attention, I see I have yours." She smiled coyly. "I can be a bright star." She beamed her light at him for a split second causing Follin to close his eyes and put his hand up to stop her luminosity from blinding him. "Or I can be a wolf." Now The Star was a ferocious wolf, she growled at him and again Follin reacted, this time in fear.

"OK, OK!" he stammered, "I give in, please, stay naked if you will and I'll get that coat for you anyway. I'm feeling a bit uncomfortable. I've not seen many naked women you know."

The two walked to his camp fire and Follin draped his well-worn but warm coat around the shoulders of The Star.

"Follin, I came here to demonstrate that accessing a sense of 'hopefulness' is part of your learning on this journey. The 'hope' I speak of is that of the meaningfulness of your journey. Despite the discomfort of your experience in the tavern, your meeting with Death and the shock of The Tower, you can still go within to find peace, harmony and hope. My Star above you illuminates your ascent upwards and onwards."

"I don't understand, I thought that hope was just that – hope," replied the youth.

"I think I need to use the same technique my friend Pan used. Please, close your eyes, meld with me and I'll demonstrate what I am trying to tell you." The Starwoman glowed from within. Follin felt himself drawn into her body.

The joy he felt was almost overwhelming; not only joy but he actually felt hopeful that his journey to discover himself would come to an end. Follin now believed with all his heart that he would achieve his goal – to be free of the stagnation of his past and find the meaning of his existence.

"I can feel the water beneath one foot and the earth beneath the other. It's a wonderful balance." Follin paused to experience more. "I can now feel the water you are pouring onto both the earth and the sea." Follin laughed with joy at the insights he was receiving. "You're using a secret alchemical process which allows hope to flourish in this world. You're doing magic, I think it has to do with peace, harmony and unity..."

"You really are doing well, young man. Now let me lift my eyes and tell me what I am seeing."

"I see starlight, like a pathway or a stairway - and it leads to heaven!" he announced with joy. "Wow, this is beauty indeed. So that's why you were naked, to show me the beauty and magical alchemy of balancing the elements. But what is this stairway to the stars, is that really heaven?" asked Follin.

"It's whatever you want heaven to be. If you want you can walk the stairs with me and take a look," challenged The Star.

"Oh yeah! I'd like that!" Follin was still in raptures from The Star's energy. He could clearly feel it flowing powerfully through his body.

As one being they walked the stairway to heaven. He already knew that The Star was one of the first celestial beings created after the birth of the universe. Through her he would experience firsthand this meeting with the very source of creation. In the space of a heartbeat Follin felt an awakening, an insight into the plan formed by Pan and the other gods. Together they had created planet Earth and many other habitable planets. Theirs was not to dominate but rather to experience, to fulfil a burning curiosity to understand the meaning of life themselves through their creations.

What Follin experienced in heaven caused him to fill with joy and power. It overwhelmed him, so much so that he collapsed into a state of deep unconsciousness. It was time for The Star to bring her apprentice home, back to his bed under her canopy of stars.

The next morning he awoke and thought to himself, *'The beautiful Star-lady proved to me that there is a purpose and meaning to this arduous mystic's path. She has given me hope and a realisation that what I am doing is not an illusion, that there is a magical world beyond the mundane existence I once thought was normal.'* Follin smiled to himself, *'Maybe The Star can show me the way home to my Lover, Eve...'*

Follin pondered for a moment longer, *'She said that she was there to give the mystic a boost of energy to help them in the final stages of their journey. That must mean I am close to the end of my journey.'* He continued to contemplate his meeting with The Star as he packed his camping gear into his bag and prepared to tidy his campsite.

It was not until he was back walking along the forest path that he remembered all he had experienced the night before. *'I wonder... did I really visit heaven?'*

The Moon

Disillusionment; deceit; lies; misinformation; nightmare; irrational fears; disguise; betrayal; abandonment; delusion; fantasy; dreams; visions; lunacy; distractions.

From The Pictorial Key to the Tarot A.E. Waite (1911)

"The card represents life of the imagination apart from life of the spirit. The path between the towers is the issue into the unknown. The dog and wolf are the fears of the natural mind in the presence of that place of exit, when there is only reflected light to guide it."

~

Follin returned to walking the forest paths feeling the joyfulness and elevated energy raised by his meeting with The Star. One evening, while sitting at his campfire and contemplating The Star's message, he saw a bright, full moon, rising on the darkening horizon. Suddenly he felt an urgent need to sleep. He made up his camp bed and settled down for an early night.

As he drifted off to sleep the moonlight grew so bright that it dominated his unconscious mind. He dreamed that he floated on a moonbeam, upwards towards The Moon. There he saw two dogs. One appeared to be a wolf, but it did not seem to be as fierce as The Star's manifestation a few months ago. The other was a domestic dog. Neither took much notice of him - but they certainly made a noise as they barked and bayed incessantly. The sound was eerie and disconcerting. It disturbed Follin's mind and he struggled to concentrate on his visions.

He quaked in fright when he spied a scorpion stalking towards him. There was no order, nor rhyme nor reason for the things he was seeing. These were hallucinations; strange, unclear images and noises causing a mixture of feelings to arise inside him. Follin felt a deep regret, it tormented him. There appeared a series of happy visions too, moments of love and joyfulness that he struggled to hold on to, but they were soon ripped away from him.

'I must be having a nightmare. If it stays like this it's going to drive me mad. I'll turn into a lunatic if I stay inside this crazy dream.' As each vision crossed his mind he reeled in confusion.

'I feel as though these illusions are trying to conceal something, like a dishonest person trying to disguise the truth. It's all distorted, there is no truth, no honour here, it's just trying to distract me from my real purpose. I need to take a step back and leave this nightmare.'

Forcing himself awake Follin realised that this was like Pan's test. He had visited a world of fantasy, of distractions and illusions that could have frightened him and caused him to turn from his path. Remembering his conversation with The Star he recognised that these dreams were not real and that he must resume his journey.

The Sun

Happiness; enlightenment; vitality; youth; friendship; enthusiasm; an honest victory.

From The Pictorial Key to the Tarot A.E. Waite (1911)

"The card signifies ... the transit from the manifest light of this world, represented by the glorious sun of earth, to the light of the world to come, which goes before aspiration and is typified by the heart of a child... The characteristic type of humanity has become a little child therein - a child in the sense of simplicity and innocence in the sense of wisdom. In that simplicity, he bears the seal of Nature and of Art; in that innocence, he signifies the restored world..."

~

The morning birthed bright. The Sun kindly warmed the youth's exhausted body. Follin prepared to break his fast as he enjoyed the smiling Sun above. Looking around, he saw he was under a tall shady tree in a splendid garden with many types of flowers. It filled him with wonder for, indeed, it was a beautiful day. When he had fallen asleep the night before he was sure he was in an empty, desolate wasteland. But now he had awoken to see a garden filled with well-tended roses, grape vines, enormous sunflowers and many flowering plants he did not recognise.

There was something about The Sun that reminded Follin of The Star and The Empress. Then it struck him, The Sun represented Fire, that created energy and life. This was the energy brought about by hope and meaningfulness that The Star had explained to him.

'What if I meditate on The Sun or fire and see what happens? I remember my father telling me that he sometimes used the campfire for his meditations. I was always afraid to ask him how to do it because I feared he would tell me to walk into the fire. But feeling the sunshine I think I know how to do it.'

He sat in front of his campfire in the shade and quietened his mind as he had been taught by the many mentors he had met on his journey. He looked into the campfire with soft eyes and imagined he was stepping into the flames.

'Yes! This is what The Empress and The Star were so generous to show me, the lesson was of fire energy and now I can do it myself, I don't need their help anymore.'

With a slow, deep breath Follin felt the flames enter his body burning away the fatigue, confusion and sadness that had lingered since his encounter with The Moon. As the flames reached his head he could feel himself burst out of his body and race towards The Sun.

The feeling of heat was so great that he started to burn as his body reached overload – the meditation had pushed him beyond his capacity. At this point his body wisdom shut his meditation down and he fell asleep in front of his campfire.

When he awoke Follin felt a sense of wonder that he had not felt since he was a small child. This entire experience of the fire meditation, the beautiful garden and the happiness he felt, made him feel renewed and ready to embrace the next challenge on his mystic's journey.

He laughed with delight as he saw a young boy ride towards him on a large, white horse. The boy was surrounded by an aura of flames. Follin watched in admiration as the boy and his horse performed intricate manoeuvres, while maintaining perfect balance. Follin was sure the boy smiled directly at him, just before he disappeared.

Leaving the garden with a broad smile on his face and a skip in his step, Follin felt that nothing could stop him now. He recalled his childhood, of the days when he was sad and how he would climb the tall pine trees at the back of the schoolyard to reach up to the sky itself. Up there in the tree tops he would will the sunlight to enter his body. It made him glow with joy as he felt released of the drudgery of his existence. The boy on the horse reminded Follin of how climbing the tall pine trees made him feel – happy and carefree.

After a few paces, he halted and turned for a final look at the garden - but it was gone like it had never existed. With a renewed strength of faith and conviction, Follin turned to continue on his mystic's journey.

Judgement
Be prepared; a call to arms; evaluation; redemption; release of guilt and remorse; self-forgiveness.

From <u>The Pictorial Key to the Tarot</u> A.E. Waite (1911)

"It should be noted that all the figures are as one in the wonder, adoration and ecstasy expressed by their attitudes. It is the card which registers the accomplishment of the great work of transformation in answer to the summons of the Supernal - which summons is heard and answered from within... Let the card continue to depict, for those who can see no further, the Last Judgement and the resurrection in the natural body; but let those who have inward eyes look and discover therewith. They will understand that it has been called truly in the past a card of eternal life, and for this reason it may be compared with that which passes under the name of Temperance."

~

As he walked through the forest Follin's thoughts wandered to the good times on his journey so far, especially of how much he longed to see his Lover, Eve. It was now many years since they had met and formed their bond of love. Although it had seemed an illusion at the time, he was now certain he was destined to marry this girl of his dreams. Now he was impatient to finish his quest and make a home with her.

As he walked he was startled by a tremendous blast of a trumpet, the trumpet of The Last Judgement.

The skies above began to boil and out from the clouds appeared an Angel, a giant trumpet to his lips. The trumpet blasted again and thoughts of his past sins tormented Follin's mind. He struggled to escape the terrible guilt that invaded him with each blast. Then, in a flash of insight, he recalled the teachings of his mentors.

Follin remembered how he had worked so hard to heal his past. When he had lived as a hermit in solitude in the small mossy cottage, his inner child had come to play with him and was healed. Follin had learned from his life experiences and from his mentors, to go with the flow and not against it – this was his mystic path and now he was ready for this, his Day of Judgement.

If Judgement was about to judge him for all that he had failed to do and for the wrongful things that he had done, then Follin was ready.

With growing confidence Follin cried out to the Angel above, "I am no longer a slave to my past, now I am master of my future. If I am destined to die this day then let it be so. I am prepared to meet my end." In that moment Follin forgave himself his failings, real and imagined. He let go of his fears and expectations *"...and I am good enough!"* he bellowed - the trumpet blasts suddenly died away.

Silence pervaded the forest once again and Follin, the mystic, continued on his journey through the Tarot Empire.

The World

The final outcome; achievement; completion; unity; overview; fulfilment; a pure accomplishment.

From <u>The Pictorial Key to the Tarot</u> A.E. Waite (1911)

"It represents also the perfection and end of the Cosmos, the secret which is within it, the rapture of the universe when it understands itself in God. It is further the state of the soul in the consciousness of Divine Vision, reflected from the self-knowing spirit... The figure has been said to stand for Truth, which is, however, more properly allocated to the seventeenth card. Lastly, it has been called the Crown of the Magi."

~

Follin had finally found peace within his heart. For the first time on his journey he felt whole. He hummed an old village ballad as he prepared his evening meal of beans and the vegetables he had collected on his path that day. He drew a pouch from inside his warm coat and added the contents to his pot. Having lived on the road for so long he knew exactly which herbs to collect, what flavour they imparted, and to what meal he could add them.

'This is such a beautiful place. The river is calm, there's a village not too far away. It has a tavern where I'm sure to get some work and earn enough to buy more food, maybe I'll get these boots repaired too. I might even spend a few weeks here before heading home, to Eve.' Follin directed his thoughts to the trees and the bubbling river as it swept over the stones beside his campsite.

That evening he meditated, as was his habit before he retired for the night. This night he felt that life was as it should be - complete. Even his longing to be reunited with Eve was complete within itself.

The patterns of light and shadow played against the tree trunks and branches around his campfire. It felt like everything around him was alive and shared in his happiness.

It was at that moment of feeling so happy his heart would break, that the ground began to shudder; it felt like he was in the middle of an earthquake. An enormous wheel spun in his mind, like the world itself was spinning.

Follin felt himself spinning too – in perfect harmony with The World. *'All is right with The World and I am happy'* were his last thoughts as he fell, still spinning that perfect spin, into a deep and dreamless sleep.

Epilogue

Follin awoke to the familiar scent of the sea. The light breeze carried memories of his childhood and the happy times with his father on their trips to the beaches near their village. *'I must be closer to the sea than I realised'*, he thought.

He could just see the yellow of the sand dunes beyond the edge of the forest. By now he had learned to trust his instincts and his thoughts once again turned toward his home across the sea, to the Mystic Isle he had left so long ago.

By now Follin was so immersed in the daily habits of caring for his immediate needs that he lit a fire and prepared to break his fast with a bowel of barley oats. He brushed the sand and leaves off his clothes, washed and repacked his breakfast utensils and then decided what he should do next.

Lifting his gaze towards the sea he became aware of a growing urgency to get up and race towards his home, the Mystic Isle, but self-discipline steadied him as he put out his campfire and said a final farewell to the forest that he had come to know so well. Follin knew in his heart that he had finally arrived at the destination of his mystic's journey in the Tarot Empire. He shouldered his staff and bundle, stood up tall, then softly, gently followed the path down to the seashore.

As he crested the final dune, Follin saw a group of people moving as one toward him along the beach. He paused, shielding his eyes from the bright sunlight. As they approached he thought he recognised The Magician, The Charioteer and other mystical personages from his time in the Tarot Empire, but scarcely dared to hope that it was indeed them.

As they drew near, he heard their voices but could only hear snippets of what sounded like singing; a melody that tugged at his heartstrings and brought tears of remembrance to his eyes. Through his blurred vision he made out individual faces and heard individual voices blending, weaving. Gradually, as they moved closer, he realised that they were singing of him, a ballad of his adventures and of his interactions with each of them.

They formed a semicircle around him and, as the melody faded away, one by one they came forward and touched him forehead to forehead then rejoined the others. Follin's heart swelled. Waves of feeling swept through him; pride quickly gave way to humility; joy and gratitude became ecstasy then faded to quietude and peace. With each forehead touch Follin felt the essence of each of them and memories of their time together flooded through his mind.

The last to come forward was The Magician. He took Follin's hands in his as he stepped back and looked into Follin's eyes. "Do you have any final questions?" he asked gently.

"When you met me at the beach, so long ago...how many years since then?"

"You have journeyed for seven years," smiled The Magician.

"Your gifts, I haven't used them..."

"No, but you have learned how to use them. When the time comes, and it will as the mystic's journey has no ending, you will be called upon to study them in each of the Tarot Kingdoms. You will learn to use them wisely, to benefit not only yourself but others, for the greatest good."

"But why me? Why did you choose me?"

"Remember the scarecrow? We saw that you gave him your shirt, without expectation of reward or any other gain. You did not know that anyone was watching. Some would say how foolish. We truly saw your generosity of spirit and we made a worthy choice. We saw that you were ready to begin your journey."

The Magician gently released Follin's hands and stepped backwards. He drew himself up to his full height and in a loud, formal voice announced:

"Follin: you are no longer the fool you thought you were. You are now a wiser young man, who can embrace both your foolishness and your wisdom. To us alone you are The Fool, our Fool."

The Magician then pointed behind Follin who turned to see a rainbow stretching far across the sea. When he turned around again he was alone. With a full heart and a clear mind Follin picked up his possessions and softly, gently, stepped onto the rainbow bridge.

~

Follin was once more at the door of his parent's house from which he had fled seven years earlier. Back then he had been a frightened and depressed youth of fourteen.

The young man now found himself in a state of contentment and great expectation. He was different, he felt an overwhelming sense of wholeness. Follin could not wait to share his stories and newfound knowledge with his family and friends - with everyone.

Follin withdrew from his reverie when he heard a familiar voice. It sent shivers of excitement up his spine. He turned towards the voice and there, running towards him, was the blonde-haired woman he had met and fallen in love with long ago.

It was his Lover, Eve, with a smile on her face and laughter in her voice. Follin was home at last and felt a fool no more.

The journey continues.....

The Fool's Journey through the Tarot
✪ Pentacles ✪

Noel Eastwood

Book 2 The Fool's Journey Series

The Fool's Journey through the Tarot
— Swords —

Noel Eastwood

Book 3 The Fool's Journey Series

About the author

Noel Eastwood is a recently retired Psychologist with over forty years combined professional experience in education, counselling and psychology. Now a full-time author, Noel shares his lifelong interests in Taoist meditation, Tai Chi, Astrology and Tarot. A gifted storyteller, his fiction and nonfiction works blend ancient wisdom and contemporary themes.

Publications

*The Fool's Journey through the Tarot **Major Arcana***
3rd Edition 2018 - Book 1 The Fool's Journey Series

*The Fool's Journey through the Tarot **Pentacles** 2018*
- Book 2 The Fool's Journey Series

*The Fool's Journey through the Tarot **Swords** 2018*
- Book 3 The Fool's Journey Series

(Book 4 ***"Cups"*** and Book 5 ***"Wands"*** of The Fool's Journey Series will be published later in 2018)

Psychological Astrology and the Twelve Houses

Astrology of Health: Physical and Psychological Health in the Natal and Progressed Charts

Tame your Inner Dragons: Clinical and Psychic Use of Trance

Available at all online bookstores

Website

You can visit Noel Eastwood's website and subscribe to his newsletters at www.plutoscave.com

Reviews

"In October of 2009 Carl Jung's Red Book was released for the first time. Chronicling the great psychoanalyst's venture into his own subconscious, revealing fractal universes and personifications of unconscious material. A whole new world of it's own. One that is not unlike the universal symbology embodied in the Major Arcana of the Tarot. Noel Eastwood's delightful book, "The Fool's Journey through the Tarot Major Arcana," *is unlike any other tool for learning about this centuries old symbology and how it can be meditated upon, and used to relate to the workings of our daily lives, and our own subconscious. It is a free-flowing, progressive adventure of the Fool through all of the other cards. Taking the simple Spirit he was conceived with, the Fool advances as he encounters each force and personality. A true 'Hero's Journey,' and one that every spiritual adventurist will love and recognize. The story sucked me in, and only spat me out at the end. I recommend this series as a companion to the works of Carl Jung, Anna Wise, Joseph Campbell, Paul Foster Case, J. Nigro Sansonese, and my own."* FK

"I've read many of Noel's books on Astrology and tarot. I'm always amazed at how easily his writings lend themselves to being transformative to readers at any point along the Tao.
His writings present the reader with a systematic approach to psychological and spiritual growth little matched in understanding and ease of use, than by any other writers I can think of.
If you are looking for a place to begin or enrich your journey, I'd recommend you follow the Fool in his journey through the Tarot." MR

"What a wonderful way to bring an easy and deep understanding of the major arcana. This book was enlightening and entertaining from start to finish. I'm definitely not a tarot student, or teacher. Far from it. But this book makes me want to learn. A whole new world has opened up for me. It's an odd feeling having epiphanies as I read, but that happened. Beautifully written and drawn, The Fool's Journey is a keeper!" KM

"This easy to understand text is not in any way simplistic; it's filled with deep meaning. This book will assist in your inward journey. Use it along with meditation to reach a better understanding of yourself and others." MR

"I really loved this book, I will be buying book 2 and 3 of this series for sure. As I was reading it helped me to reflect on my life and when I've been at each card, it gave a lot of deeper meanings and shed some light on some of the cards I don't love to see when pulling for myself. Not only that, it truly kept me captivated and interested to see how Follin felt after getting to the World card. Can't wait for his journey through the Pentacles." C

"A magical journey through the tarot! Delightful to read - also, makes the tarot cards easier to learn/remember. I highly recommend this series - whether you are a beginner or advanced tarot reader." AC

www.ingramcontent.com/pod-product-compliance
Lightning Source LLC
Chambersburg PA
CBHW072052290426
44110CB00014B/1648

As if